Pebble
Bilingüe/
Bilingual

Algunos niños usan sillas de ruedas / Some Kids Use Wheelchairs

por/by Lola M. Schaefer

Editor Consultor/Consulting Editor: Dra. Gail Saunders-Smith

Consultor/Consultant: Nancy Dobson, Director
Pediatric Therapy Services, Mankato, Minnesota

CAPSTONE PRESS
a capstone imprint

Pebble Books are published by Capstone Press,
151 Good Counsel Drive, P.O. Box 669, Mankato, Minnesota 56002.
www.capstonepress.com

092009
005618CGS10

 Books published by Capstone Press are manufactured with paper
containing at least 10 percent post-consumer waste.

Library of Congress Cataloging-in-Publication Data
Schaefer, Lola M., 1950–
    [Some kids use wheelchairs. Spanish]
    Algunos niños usan sillas de ruedas / por Lola M. Schaefer = Some kids use
wheelchairs / by Lola M. Schaefer.
    p. cm. — (Understanding differences = Comprendiendo las diferencias)
    Includes index.
    Summary: "Simple text and photographs discuss why some kids cannot walk, how
wheelchairs help them, and the everyday activities of children who use wheelchairs — in
both English and Spanish" — Provided by publisher.
    ISBN 978-1-4296-4592-8 (library binding)
    1. People with disabilities — Transportation — Juvenile literature. 2. People with
disabilities — Orientation and mobility — Juvenile literature. 3. Children with disabilities
— Transportation — Juvenile literature. 4. Children with disabilities — Orientation and
mobility — Juvenile literature. 5. Wheelchairs — Juvenile literature. I. Title. II. Title: Some
kids use wheelchairs. III. Series.
HV3022.S3318 2010
362.4'3 — dc22   2009030379

Note to Parents and Teachers

The Comprendiendo las diferencias/Understanding Differences set supports national
social studies standards related to individual development and identity. This book
describes and illustrates the special needs of children who use wheelchairs in both
English and Spanish. The photographs support early readers in understanding the
text. The repetition of words and phrases helps early readers learn new words. This
book also introduces early readers to subject-specific vocabulary words, which are
defined in the Glossary. Early readers may need assistance to read some words and
to use the Table of Contents, Glossary, Internet Sites, and Index sections of the book.

Table of Contents

Tabla de contenidos

Why Kids Use Wheelchairs

Some kids use wheelchairs. Kids who cannot walk use wheelchairs to go places.

¿Por qué algunos niños usan sillas de ruedas?

Algunos niños usan sillas de ruedas. Los niños que no pueden caminar usan sillas de ruedas para ir a diferentes lugares.

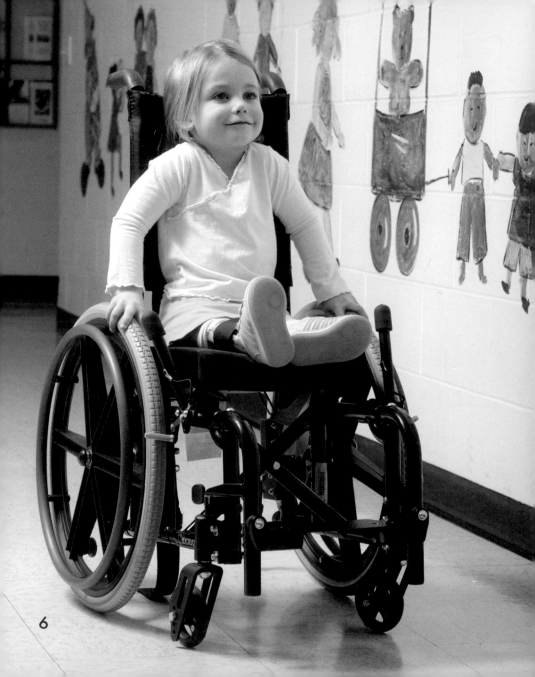

Some kids cannot walk because they were born with weak bones or muscles. Other kids use a wheelchair after they get hurt.

Algunos niños no pueden caminar porque nacieron con huesos o músculos débiles. Otros niños usan una silla de ruedas después de lastimarse.

Some kids who use wheelchairs go swimming. The exercise is good for their muscles.

Algunos niños que usan sillas de ruedas nadan. El ejercicio es bueno para sus músculos.

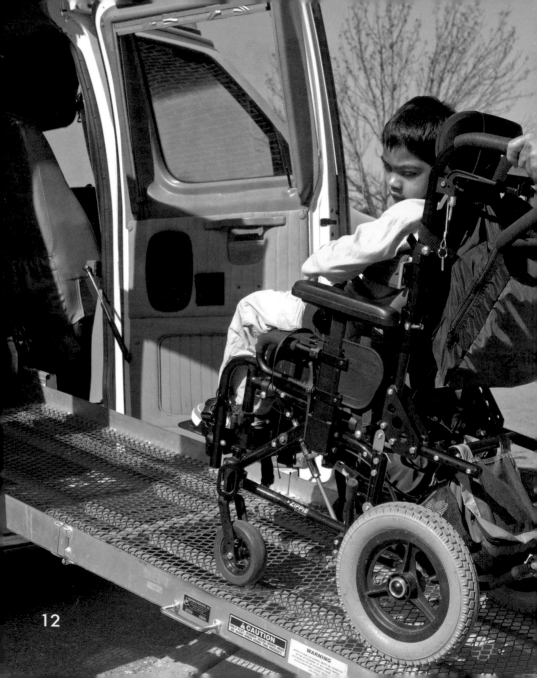

Everyday Life

Kids who use wheelchairs go many places. They use ramps to get into vans.

La vida diaria

Los niños que usan sillas de ruedas van a muchos lugares. Usan rampas para subir a camionetas.

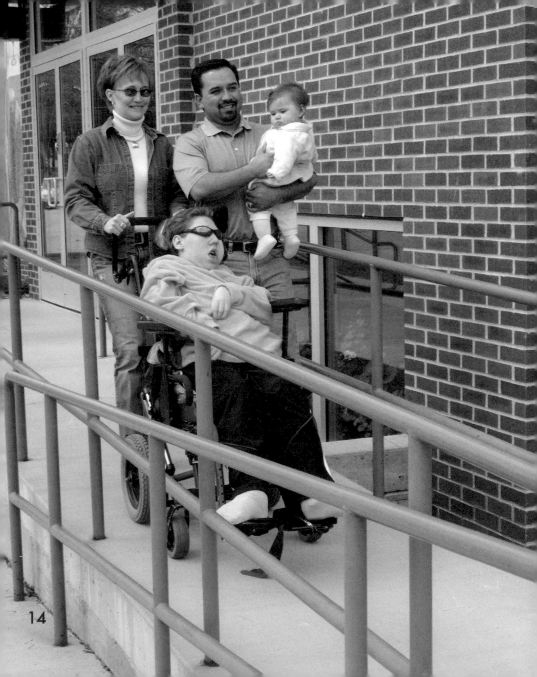

They use ramps to enter
and exit buildings.

Ellos usan rampas para
entrar y salir de edificios.

Kids who use wheelchairs
go to the library. They read
books and use computers.

Los niños que usan
sillas de ruedas van a
la biblioteca. Ellos leen
libros y usan computadoras.

Some kids who use
wheelchairs play sports.
They like to have fun.

Algunos niños que usan sillas
de ruedas practican deportes.
A ellos les gusta divertirse.

Some kids who use wheelchairs go to camp. They follow trails through the woods.

Algunos niños que usan sillas de ruedas van de campamento. Ellos siguen los senderos a través del bosque.

Glossary

physical therapist — a person trained to give treatment to people who are hurt or have physical disabilities; massage and exercise are two kinds of treatment.

ramp — a flat area that slants to connect two levels; ramps allow people in wheelchairs to get into buildings and vans.

wheelchair — a type of chair on wheels for people who are ill, hurt, or have physical disabilities; wheelchairs can be pushed by hand or by motor.

Internet Sites

FactHound offers a safe, fun way to find Internet sites related to this book. All of the sites on FactHound have been researched by our staff.

Here's how:

Visit *www.facthound.com*

FactHound will fetch the best sites for you!

Glosario

el fisioterapeuta — una persona capacitada para dar tratamiento a personas con lesiones o que tienen discapacidades físicas; masajes y ejercicios son dos tipos de tratamiento.

la rampa — un área plana inclinada para conectar dos niveles; las rampas permiten a las personas en sillas de ruedas ingresar a edificios y camionetas.

la silla de ruedas — un tipo de silla sobre ruedas para personas que están enfermas, lesionadas o que tienen discapacidades físicas; las sillas de ruedas pueden ser empujadas manualmente o por un motor.

Sitios de Internet

FactHound brinda una forma segura y divertida de encontrar sitios de Internet relacionados con este libro. Todos los sitios en FactHound han sido investigados por nuestro personal.

Esto es todo lo que tú necesitas hacer:

Visita *www.facthound.com*

¡FactHound buscará los mejores sitios para ti!

Index

Índice

Editorial Credits

Strictly Spanish, translation services; Katy Kudela, bilingual editor; Bob Lentz, designer; Eric Manske, production specialist

Photo Credits

Capstone Press/Karon Dubke, 6, 12, 14, 16; Getty Images Inc./Taxi, cover; Gregg R. Andersen, 8; Marilyn Moseley LaMantia, 20; Muscular Dystrophy Association, 4, 10, 18